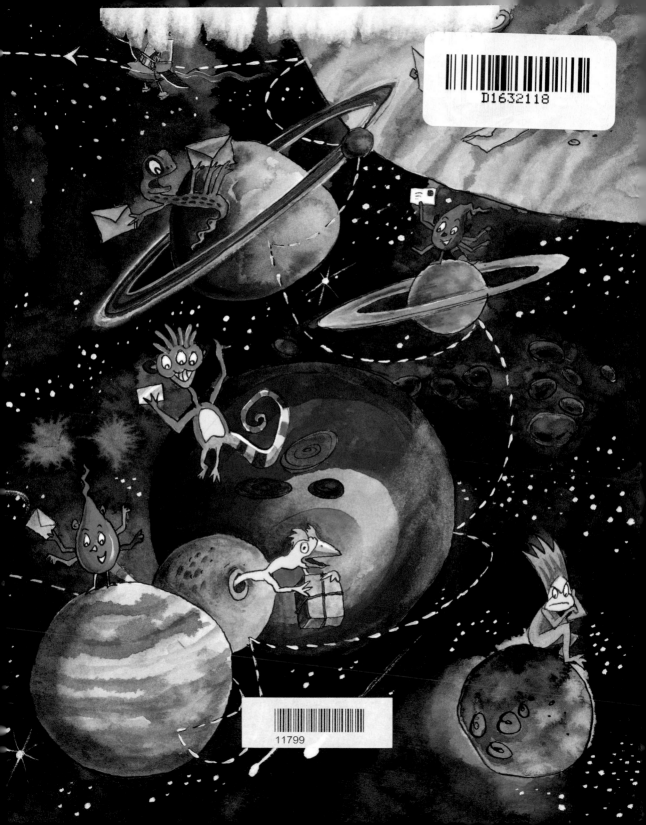

To parents and teachers

We hope you and the children will enjoy reading this story in either English or French. The story is simple, but not *simplified* so the language of the French and the English is quite natural but there is lots of repetition.

At the back of the book is a small picture dictionary with the key words and how to pronounce them. There is also a simple pronunciation guide to the whole story on the last page.

Here are a few suggestions on using the book:

• Read the story aloud in English first, to get to know it. Treat it like any other picture book: look at the pictures, talk about the story and the characters and so on.

• Then look at the picture dictionary and say the French names for the key words. Ask the children to repeat them. Concentrate on speaking the words out loud, rather than reading them.

• Go back and read the story again, this time in English *and* French. Don't worry if your pronunciation isn't quite correct. Just have fun trying it out. Check the guide at the back of the book, if necessary, but you'll soon pick up how to say the French words.

• When you think you and the children are ready, you can try reading the story in French only. Ask the children to say it with you. Only ask them to read it if they are keen to try. The spelling could be confusing and put them off.

• Above all encourage the children to have a go and give lots of praise. Little children are usually quite unselfconscious and this is excellent for building up confidence in a foreign language.

Published by b small publishing
The Book Shed, 36 Leyborne Park, Kew, Richmond, Surrey, TW9 3HA, UK
www.bsmall.co.uk
© b small publishing, 2005
1 2 3 4 5
All rights reserved.
Design: *Lone Morton and Louise Millar*   Editorial: *Catherine Bruzzone and Susan Martineau*
Production: *Madeleine Ehm*
Colour reproduction: *Vimnice Printing Press Co. Ltd.* Printed in China by *WKT Co. Ltd.*
ISBN-13: 9781902915173   ISBN-10: 1-902915-17-8 (UK French hardback)
British Library Cataloguing in Publication Data. A catalogue record for this book is available from the British Library.

Space postman

Le facteur spatial

Lone Morton

Pictures by Martin Ursell
French by Marie-Thérèse Bougard

b small publishing

Captain Crater climbs
into his spaceship.
He is the space postman.

Le capitaine Crater monte
dans son engin spatial.
Il est facteur spatial.

He turns the blue dial to the left

Il tourne la manette bleue à gauche

and the yellow dial to the right.

et la manette jaune à droite.

He presses the green button:

Il appuie sur le bouton vert:

GO!
PARTEZ!

BLAST OFF!

C'EST LE LANCEMENT!

Whoosh! He takes off into the sky.

Zoum! Il s'en va dans le ciel.

His first stop is Planet Fizz.
He has a letter for Princess Shush.

Son premier arrêt est la planète Fizz.
Il a une lettre pour la Princesse Shush.

It's an invitation to a wedding.
She is very happy.

C'est une invitation à un mariage.
Elle est très contente.

Second stop: Planet Ooloo.
He has a parcel for Farmer Flop.

Deuxième arrêt: la planète Oulou.
Il a un colis pour Flop, le fermier.

It's a big book.
He is very happy.

C'est un grand livre.
Il est très content.

Next stop is Planet Astro.
He has a postcard for Blop.

Le prochain arrêt est la planète Astro.
Il a une carte postale pour Blop.

Oh, no!
Oh, non!

On the way, the door opens…
En route la porte s'ouvre…

…and the post bag falls out!
…et le sac postal tombe!

Captain Crater lands on Planet Astro.
But there is no post bag.

Le capitaine Crater se pose
sur la planète Astro.
Mais il n'y pas de sac postal.

"I am going to look for it," he says to Blop. "But I will come back."

"Je vais aller le chercher", dit-il à Blop. "Mais je reviens."

He flies east.
Il va à l'est.

He flies west.
Il va à l'ouest.

He flies north and then south.
Il va au nord et puis au sud.

But he can't find the post bag anywhere.

Mais il ne trouve le sac postal nulle part.

"Bleep, bleep, bleep," his phone rings.

"Blip, blip, blip", son téléphone sonne.

"Hello, hello. It's the space police."
"We have found a post bag...

"Allô, allô. C'est la police spatiale."
"Nous avons trouvé un sac postal...

...hanging from a star!"

...accroché à une étoile!"

Captain Crater is very happy.

Le capitaine Crater est très content.

Blop's postcard is from his twin brother, Blip.

La carte postale de Blop
vient de son frère jumeau, Blip.

"He's arriving tomorrow on the
Space Bus!"
Blop is very happy.

"Il arrive demain par le bus spatial!"
Blop est très content.

Pronouncing French

Don't worry if your pronunciation isn't quite correct. The important thing is to be willing to try. The pronunciation guide here will help but it cannot be completely accurate:

• Read the guide as naturally as possible, as if it were British English.

• Put stress on the letters in *italics*, e.g. fak-*ter*.

• Don't roll the r at the end of the word, for example in the French word **le** (the): ler.

If you can, ask a French person to help and move on as soon as possible to speaking the words without the guide.

Note French adjectives usually have two forms, one for masculine and one for feminine nouns, e.g. **content** and **contente.**

Words Les mots

leh moh

star

l'étoile

let*wal*

sky

le ciel

ler see-*el*

spaceship

l'engin spatial

lon*jah* spah-see-*al*

space bus

le bus spatial

ler boos spah-see-*al*

postman
le facteur
ler fak-*ter*

post bag
le sac postal
ler sak post*al*

postcard
la carte postal
lah kart post*al*

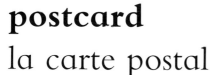

happy
content,
contente
kon*toh*, kon*tont*

parcel
le colis
ler ko*lee*

letter
la lettre
lah letr'

big
grand, grande
groh, grond

book
le livre
ler leevr'

north

nord
nor

west

ouest
oowest

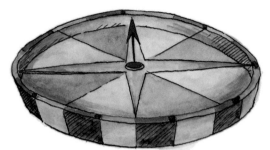

east

est
est

south

sud
sood

left

gauche
goh-sh

right

droite
drwat

blue

bleu, bleue
bl', bl'

yellow

jaune
shown

green

vert, verte
vair, vairt

A simple guide to pronouncing this French story

Le facteur spatial
ler fak-*ter* spah-see-*al*

Le capitaine Crater monte dans son engin spatial.
ler kapee-*ten* krat-*air* mont doh soh an*jah* spah-see-*al*

Il est facteur spatial.
eel eh fak-*ter* spah-see-*al*

Il tourne la manette bleue à gauche
eel too-rn lah man*et* bl' ah goh-sh

et la manette jaune à droite.
eh lah man*et* shown ah drwat

Il appuie sur le bouton vert:
eel ap*wee* s-yoor ler boo*toh* vair

PARTEZ!
par-*teh*

C'EST LE LANCEMENT!
seh ler lons-*moh*

Zoum! Il s'en va dans le ciel.
zoom, eel soh va doh ler see-*el*

Son premier arrêt est la planète Fizz.
soh premee-*eh* a*reh* teh lah pla*net* feez

Il a une lettre pour la Princesse Shush.
eel ah y-oon letr' poor lah prah-*sess* shoosh

C'est une invitation à un mariage.
seh toon ahn-vee-tah-see-*oh* ah ahn maree-*aj*

Elle est très contente.
el eh treh kon*tont*

Deuxième arrêt: la planète Oulou
der-zee-*em* a*reh* lah pla*net* oo*loo*

Il a un colis pour Flop, le fermier.
eel ah ahn ko*lee* poor flop, ler fairm-ee-*eh*

C'est un grand livre.
set ahn groh leevr'

Il est très content.
eel eh treh kon*toh*

Le prochain arrêt est la planète Astro.
ler pro*shah* a*reh* eh lah pla*net* as*tro*

Il a une carte postale pour Blop.
eel ah yoon kart pos*tal* poor blop

Oh, non! En route la porte s'ouvre…
oh noh, ahn root lah port soovr'

…et le sac postal tombe!
eh ler sak pos*tal* tomb

Le capitaine Crater se pose
ler kapee-*ten* krat-*air* ser pose

sur la planète Astro.
soor lah pla*net* astro

Mais il n'y a pas de sac postal.
meh eel nee ah pah der sak pos*tal*

"Je vais aller le chercher", dit-il à Blop.
sher vay a*leh* ler shair-*sheh* deet-eel ah blop

"Mais je reviens."
meh sher rer-vee*ah*

Il va à l'est. Il va à l'ouest.
eel vah ah lest, eel va ah loo*west*

Il va au nord et puis au sud.
eel va oh nor, pwee oh sood

Mais il ne trouve le sac postal
meh eel troov pah ler sak pos*tal*

nulle part.
nool pah

"Blip, blip, blip", son téléphone sonne.
bleep, bleep, bleep, soh teh-leh-*foh* son

"Allô, allô. C'est la police spatiale."
allo, allo, seh lah po*lees* spah-see-*al*

"Nous avons trouvé un sac postal…"
noo za*voh* troo*veh* ahn sak pos*tal*

…accroché à une étoile!
…akro*sheh* ah oon et-*wal*

Le capitaine Crater est très content.
ler kapee-*ten* krat-*air* eh treh kon*toh*

La carte postale de Blop
lah kart pos*tal* der blop

vient de son frère jumeau, Blip.
vee-*ah* der soh frair shoo*moh* bleep

"Il arrive demain par le bus spatial!"
eel a*reev* der-mah par ler boos spah-see-*al*

Blop est très content.
blop eh treh kon*toh*